# The Habit of Hope

*is a Path Book*
*offering practical spirituality*
*to enrich everyday living.*

*"Your word is a lamp to my feet*
*and a light to my path."*
Psalm 119:105

# The Habit
# of Hope

*In a Changing
and Uncertain World*

# William Hockin

Path Books
A LIGHT TO MY PATH

Path Books
an imprint of ABC Publishing
Anglican Book Centre
600 Jarvis Street
Toronto, Ontario M4Y 2J6

Cover design by Jane Thornton

**Canadian Cataloguing in Publication Data**

Hockin, William J.
  The habit of hope : in a changing and uncertain world

ISBN 1-55126-325-4

1. Spiritual life. 2. Hope — Religious aspects — Christianity.
3. Change — Religious aspects — Christianity.  I. Title.

BV4501.2.H57 2001      248.4      C00-933144-1

*to Joseph Frost Hockin*
*1907–1996*

# Contents

# Preface

One of my father's favourite sayings was, "The sky will soon be clearing in the west." Uttered usually at the end of a summer thunderstorm, it was always more to me than just a weather forecast. It revealed my father's habit of hope. I can recall on many occasions his deep consciousness of something better to come. It was a consciousness rooted in his faith in Jesus Christ, sustained through all his eighty-nine years. It gave his life a frame of a reference, a joy, and a profound sense of gratitude.

I confess that I have not always been that hopeful. Throughout my thirty-five years of ministry I have witnessed the downsizing of the mainline churches and a polarization of panic-driven points of view among those who remain. It's sometimes hard to see hope in the institutional church. And our secular culture, with its exaltation of the banal and the selfish, offers little in the way of hope either.

As a result of this and more, many of us live our days with a kind of low-grade cynicism that makes it easy to attack authority, resist change, find something negative to talk about, and build walls to separate ourselves from anyone who has differing opinions.

This book is written as a humble, yet serious, attempt to counter these negative pulls in our lives and in the church. It is written in the conviction that God is calling us forward. Both in the church and in our personal lives, God is to be found not only in the status quo but also on the edge of positive redemptive change. It is my hope that these chapters will illustrate for you the fact that hope is not just a personality trait given to some but, rather, a habit of life. Like all habits, we can choose to cultivate it. The biblical characters and others whom I describe made a habit of hope in their lives. Hope was something they "did" every day.

I am grateful to my father for modelling the habit of hope. It has taken me many years to catch up, but finally I have discovered that hope is something that needs to be practised every day — by prayer, by listening, by being excited with God's surprises and expectant of his daily grace. It is to the memory of my father that this book is dedicated.

# 1

# When Life Gets
# a Little Crazy

*The word that came to Jeremiah from the Lord: "Come, go down to the potter's house, and there I will let you hear my words." So I went down to the potter's house, and there he was working at his wheel.*

— Jeremiah 18:1–3

If you had moved out of a big city thirty years ago and went back now for a visit, you would hardly know your way around. Glass and steel towers have replaced old shops and houses. The familiar landmarks have been destroyed. In the countryside for miles around, farms and forests have disappeared, replaced by mile upon mile of suburbs. Traditional industries, such as farming, fishing, and forestry, are all in trouble. Similarly, the institutional framework we live in has undergone drastic changes. Social structures that used to be reliable or even predictable, like the family, church, health care, education, and work, are now in turmoil. We know the language: downsizing, revisioning, transition, post-modernism.

One of the casualties of being lost in confusing change is hope. One morning after church, a member of the parish where I had been guest preaching cornered me and started to tell her story. She was a woman in her late fifties whose husband had died two years before; she had two daughters, both divorced, now living alone with their children. "It seems that everything in life has come loose and nothing is tied down anymore."

When life gets a little crazy, what do you do?

The Bible tells us a lot about wilderness. These days, we use wilderness as a positive image: we try to preserve nature from the damage humans are inflicting on it. We see it as beautiful and unspoiled, and we retreat to it for spiritual re-creation. It's not long since our ancestors saw it as dangerous and threatening, full of the power of wild weather and animals that destroy the puny work of human hands, a place where people lose their way and get lost. The wilderness of the Bible, unlike the wilderness of Canada with its forests and lakes, was a hard stony desert. At the beginning of the twenty-first century, many of us feel that we are lost in a wild wilderness or perhaps in an urban wilderness of glass and steel.

The Bible sees wilderness as both threatening and re-creating. The children of Israel wandered forty years in the desert, often in fear and despair. Yet in the wilderness they were fed by manna, given water to drink, received God's commandments, and eventually found their way to the promised land. Moses, their leader, never lost hope. Every year in Jerusalem, the scapegoat, loaded with the sins of the people, was driven out into the wilderness, presumably to die. Yet Jesus deliberately withdrew to the wilderness to be alone and pray, certain that he would meet his Father there.

There is definitely a spiritual side to our feeling lost in the wilderness. In the last thirty years, the mainline churches have been hit hard by the confusion of rapid change. The same woman who worried that "everything in life has come loose and nothing is tied down anymore" also worried that her grandchildren weren't going to church. A lot of us are wondering: Does my faith in God work anymore? Where are my roots? We are tempted to question who we are, who God is, and even if God is. If you're feeling right now that life is a little crazy, you're not alone.

About ten years ago, when I was going through a time of feeling lost, I came across an Old Testament parable that made a lot of sense, and this reading gave me hope. It was Jeremiah 18:1–6. I found in Jeremiah a friend. Here was a man living in a very different time, but also a time when much that used to be sound, secure, and stable had "come loose and nothing was tied down anymore." Enemy armies were threatening, and Jeremiah complained that people didn't believe anything anymore, that they had lost their spiritual roots. His concerns echo an article I read in *Toronto Life* magazine entitled "How to Find Happiness in the Nineties." The author writes, "I look around me and what I see troubles me. My generation has lost its bearings.

Where once there was commitment, there is now only disenchantment. Where there was community, there is only rootlessness."

Jeremiah was feeling a little crazy when he asked God what was going on. God replied, "Come...with me to the potter's house and there I will let you hear my words." Jeremiah records that he went to the potter's house and saw him working at the wheel, "but the vessel that he was working with was marred in his hands and so the potter formed it, changed it into a different vessel as it seemed best to him." Then God said to Jeremiah, "Can I not do with you ... just as this potter does? Just like the clay in the potter's hand, so are you in my hand."

In this image of the potter, I find three reasons for profound hope. First, God is saying that what appears to us to be a world come untied, a world of meaningless and constant change, is actually a world that our God has his hands in. What appears to us to be pain and confusion is also God's hands in our lives, moulding us into more perfect vessels. We may feel that God is "high and lifted up," remotely watching us make a mess of things, then judging how we clean it up. But here we have an image of God with his hands literally in our lives.

If you've ever watched a potter, you'll know that the hands do it all. Always holding, forming, correcting, always with a plan in mind, the hands never leave the clay. According to Jeremiah, the potter keeps trying; he never abandons the clay, never lets go, never throws it out. The God of Jesus Christ holds us in the palms of his hands. When you read the New Testament and especially the gospels, you see Jesus as a very "hands-on" person.

He touches lepers, blind people, children, people who are lost in their moral and emotional wilderness. He doesn't just climb into the pulpit and preach from afar. He climbs down and touches people with hope and healing. So the first thing we see in the potter's story is that God is a "hands-on" God.

A second reason for hope comes from the phrase, "just like the clay in the potter's hand, so are you in my hand." It is an awesome thought that right now God has his hands in our lives. We're apt to think that God isn't part of "my" marriage, "my" job, "my" fear for "my" children. Instead we think God is in church, locked up in formal language in a beautiful but perhaps archaic building. But the fact is, God wants to be recognized in the here and now.

We have here a profound insight into what it is to be human. Being human is not just chemistry, not just getting sick and old and fading away. Nor is it just mind games. We're spiritual people, and even in the crazy times of our lives — especially in the crazy times of our lives — God is at work in us. True spirituality for the twenty-first century is the journey inward. It is the discovery that God is at work in our fears and memories, our hopes and dreams. Our bodies, minds, and spirits don't operate in three separate rooms. There is only one room, and in that room we "live and move and have our being."

A third insight has to do with the pain we experience when things change for us. The normal human reaction is to resist change, especially change that will disrupt our lives. The only person that really welcomes change is a wet baby. We certainly don't welcome losing a job, or separation and divorce, or moving to a place far away from family and friends. We may even have trouble with a change of job or the birth of a baby, with all the disruption such events bring. The potter suggests that God is active in the changes of our lives, not as change for the sake of change, but as change for our good, our maturity, our redemption. Change challenges us to grow — "to the measure of the full stature of Christ." Instead of resisting every change that comes our way, we can see change as God doing good things in our lives.

I remember a man in his late forties who lost his job when his firm downsized. It was a time of tremendous uncertainty for the family. They had to sell their house and eventually move into a smaller one. But he set up in business as a consultant, and although he didn't make as much money, he liked being his own boss and he had more time to spend with his growing family.

Eugene Kennedy, in his book *Free to be Human*, writes, "Endings are an aspect of that mystery that is at work in all of us all the time. Look away from it and it does not vanish. Face it and accept it and we enter more deeply into our lives and we possess our souls in a new way."

We see in the potter story a picture of God who holds us gently in his hands. In God's hands, our lives and all our situations are profoundly infused by divine purpose. The pain of change can be seen as a sign of hope leading us into God's future.

"Just like the clay ... so are you in my hand," says the Lord.

*Consider a particular pain in your life*
*that needs and receives God's healing touch.*

*What does it feel like to you*
*to be held in God's hands?*

*O Lord God, our creator,*
*steadfast as the everlasting hills*
*yet making all things new:*
*give me the courage to engage the spirit of change*
*while trusting in your eternal constancy;*
*through Christ Jesus, our Lord,*
*Redeemer of the world.*
*Amen.*

# 2

# The Agony
# and Ecstasy

*But [God] said to me, "My grace is sufficient for you, for power is made perfect in weakness. So, I will boast all the more gladly of my weaknesses, so that the power of Christ may dwell in me."*

— 2 Corinthians 12

A tremendous renewal of spiritual consciousness is happening all around us. Spirituality has become a common word, not only in church circles but in education, health care, and business as well. Several of our friends have described their recent wilderness experiences — hiking, climbing, and walking — as spiritual experiences.

Eugene Peterson writes, "There is in our time a groundswell of recognition spreading through our culture that all of life is at root spiritual. That everything we see is found and sustained by what we cannot see. Overnight, it seems, the tables are turned. Secularism has been found wanting. The soul is back" (*Christianity Today*, November 1993). The times are ripe for all sorts of spiritual experiences.

You may have heard of "Toronto Blessing," a religious phenomenon at the Airport Vineyard Church in Toronto. Many of us who visited there witnessed a highly charged religious experience — a huge crowd of people singing, waving hands in the air, falling down on the floor. For a lot of people, it set benchmarks for what Christian experience is all about, and unless they could maintain that level of ecstasy, they feared they had lost their spiritual vitality. I suspect that a lot of people think of spiritual experience this way.

During St. Paul's ministry in Corinth, he was challenged about his spiritual credentials. A contest seemed to be going on about who had the best qualifications for leadership in the church. The competition seemed to centre on who could claim the most ecstatic far-out religious high. Paul was competing against other apostles who boasted about their grand spiritual experiences. They never missed an opportunity to tell about how many hours they spent in prayer, and how God had given them gifts of tongues, prophesy, and healing. Paul knew what game they were playing, and he was tempted to match experience with experience, and gift with gift. Instead, he did something better. In his letter he says, yes, God is to be found on the mountain top, but also in the deep valleys. Yes, God is to be experienced in the ecstasy of life, but also in the agony and the weakness of life.

Paul starts with his ecstasy. He records that, fourteen years before writing his letter, he had a profound experience. He describes it as being caught up into paradise, hearing things and seeing things that no one could speak about. This experience was certainly not substance-induced. It was God's gift to Paul. He confesses that he was tempted to use this experience to give him credibility with the church. If he had started every sermon wherever he went with this story, he would have had instant credibility, power, and prestige with some. But Paul refrained, because he had another experience of God that had given him a very different rapport with people and a deeper credibility. It was not something he looked for or wanted. It was "a thorn given me in the flesh," he says.

Scholars have debated just what that this thorn was. The opinions range from poor eyesight to migraine headaches. The Greek word for "thorn" is *skolopes* — a sharp stake — obviously something that caused Paul sharp physical pain and was getting in the way of his ministry. Paul says, I prayed about it over and over again. Lord, I could do so much better for you if only I was rid of this agony. Are you not the God of healing? Please take it away. But, writes Paul, instead of receiving an instant healing (which would also sound pretty good in his next sermon), he heard God saying, "My grace is sufficient for you, for power is made perfect in weakness." The story goes that Paul never got rid of his thorn in the flesh. Instead, he learned to see it as a means of God's grace.

There's a lot here to digest. Let's go back to the essential points. First, there is for us the temptation to limit our experience of God to the positive, the upbeat, the hand-clapping experience of the exotic and wonderful. When we hear people talking about miracles and wonders, we may feel cheated, deflated, intimidated, left outside this great world of grace. Paul certainly affirms his own ecstatic experience; he also says that we find God in our weakness.

Second, all of us have our thorns in the flesh — those things that disable and devalue us in others' eyes or our own. The thorn may be a person where we live or work, a physical or emotional pain, a troubling memory. Whatever it may be, we could live a lot better without it. Maybe like Paul, we've prayed about it and it hasn't gone away. Paul makes it very clear that the thorn in the flesh does not come from God, yet with God's help it becomes for Paul a means of new strength, because he reaches out for God in a way he never otherwise would have. Paul doesn't use his thorn as a way to get sympathy. Rather, he has come to see it as a channel for God's grace. Henri Nouwen writes, "When you fully own your pain and do not expect someone to alleviate it, when you can speak about it in true freedom, then instead of being a burden for others, it becomes an encouragement and a hope."

Third, strength comes from weakness. Most of us are taught to see weakness as failure, and failure as the bitter end. We try never to admit our weaknesses. But in the New Testament, weakness — moral, physical, or emotional — is a door to God's grace. Admitting one's weakness is the first step to being open to God's power to transform us. When we can admit our faults to ourselves, to others, and to God, we hear those words, "My grace is sufficient for you," and we find that our feet are already set on the way to redemption.

Have you noticed how attracted you are to people who are secure enough to admit that they're human and that they've failed? By contrast, people who never admit that anything is wrong are rather forbidding. The secret is that, in our weakness, we lose control. God's grace takes over, and we find a strength not of ourselves. As Leonard Cohen once wrote, "There is a crack in everything. It's how the light gets in."

This is why I find Jesus of Nazareth so wonderfully attractive. He doesn't sell himself by virtue of his status or power. Instead, he is the servant washing Peter's feet, the man embracing a leper, the innocent victim hanging on the cross. His redemptive weakness attracts me. By his becoming poor, I have become rich. In *Wishful Thinking*, Frederick Buechner writes, "The Christian is one who points at Christ and says, 'I can't prove a thing. But, there's something about his eyes and his voice. There's something about the way he carries his head, his hands, the way he carries his cross, the way he carries me.' "

*Recall some high and low points in your life,*
*and how God has used them.*

*Where in you are the cracks,*
*through which the light gets in?*

❧ ❧

*O Lord, Christ Jesus,*
*who humbled yourself to be born in human likeness:*
*give me the gifts of appreciation and humility*
*to see you in all things great and small,*
*the life and promise of my soul;*
*in your name, I ask.*
*Amen.*

# 3

# When You Want to Run Away

*Now on that same day two of them were going to a village Emmaus, about seven miles from Jerusalem, and talking with each other about all these things that had happened. While they were talking and discussing, Jesus himself came near and went with them; but their eyes were kept from recognizing him.*

— Luke 24

My wife and I were once fortunate enough to own a piece of property in the country about two hours east of Toronto. I well remember the feeling of making our exit on Friday evening, when life in the city had become too much. Getting past Oshawa and seeing the hills of Northumberland County in the distance brought the promise of a brief reprieve — twenty-four hours away from the pressure and stress.

My favourite Easter story is set on the Sunday afternoon of a very long and painful weekend. Two men decided to leave the city. The death of their master on Friday afternoon, the resulting pressure, stress, fear, and anger, not to mention the rumours that he was alive after all — it was just too much. So the two of them planned to escape the city and go to Emmaus, about a three-hour walk to the west. Sunday for them was like Monday for us. Sabbath was over, and everything around them was returning to normal. It seemed impossible that either the life or death of their master would make any difference to the world at all.

I remember someone saying that all of us have been to Emmaus. Luke is the only evangelist to mention the place, and some New Testament scholars and archeologists, unable to locate it elsewhere in the gospels, have said that the road to Emmaus is the "road going nowhere." But Emmaus is whatever we do or wherever we go to make ourselves forget. Emmaus can be going to the movies, buying new clothes or a new car, watching television. It is the place we go when we are short on hope.

Right now, in these times of confusion and deep disappointment, we're clogging the road to Emmaus. Almost everybody I speak with is afflicted by work pressures, fear of unemployment, family concerns, worry about the future for their children or for the planet itself. The media produce an endless stream of reports of violence and abuse. The family, church, government, education are all institutions under threat. Even sports is full of scandal and corruption. Who or what can we trust? Is nothing sacred anymore?

American economist Robert Heilbroner, in a book called *Visions of the Future*, suggests that central to the post-modern sense of apprehension and anxiety is our loss of faith in the three great engines that powered the modern era: democratic forms of government, scientific discovery, and the capitalistic market system. No longer are we prepared to trust big government, big science, and big business. We see them now as flawed and corrupted and, having no replacements for them, we go to Emmaus.

One of the strange things about all the Easter stories is how quiet and unglamorous they are — no trumpet fanfares or waving of banners. In the Emmaus story, two ordinary men walk down a dusty road to a town that nobody has much heard of. They are aware of footsteps behind them, and a stranger invites himself into their conversation. There are no angels in the sky, no thunder from the mountains, only a stranger walking with them and breaking bread with them. Not until afterward do they realize that these ordinary events held within them the absolutely extraordinary: Jesus, their master, had walked with them.

It is on the road to Emmaus, where we spend so much of our time, that Jesus meets us. He walks with us, inviting himself into our conversation, sharing the pain of our present and our memories. He asks us questions from which we cannot escape, questions about who we are and where we're going. And if we have eyes to see and ears to hear, we recognize the stranger as Jesus, our Lord, the Son of God.

I am not a master of prayer, but perhaps there is one kind of prayer that we may have missed. In the story, Jesus listened. He didn't interrupt. All of us need times to sit quietly and tell him how it is with our lives. Perhaps in these times on our Emmaus road, we could pause for a few minutes, even an hour, find an easy chair and, in a private solitary place, tell this holy companion we call God about what's been happening. We could tell him about the Fridays of our lives — our losses, our disappointments — and why we're trying to escape along the road to Emmaus.

Then it is our turn to listen. In the story, having heard what they've been through, Jesus begins to correct some of their assumptions, turning them upside down. "Beginning at Moses and the prophets, he interpreted to them the things about himself in all the scriptures.... Why it was necessary that the Messiah should suffer these things and then enter his glory." Later on, when the disciples recalled the moment, they said, "Were not our hearts burning within us, while he was talking to us on the road, while he was opening the scriptures to us?" There are many ways to read the Bible. You can read it to get the details of the stories. You can read it to find the rules of religion. You can read it to win an argument. Or you can read it to meet Jesus — to find out what he's like and what he says.

The experience of the two disciples was that, suddenly, life started to make sense. As they listened to Jesus — the Jesus of both Friday and Sunday, the Jesus who died and rose again — some of the things that they were running away from began to change. The same can happen for us. A friend of mine, who is part of the Twelve Step Program, is often asked to share his story of recovery. He says, "Every time I tell my story, I learn something new about myself and what I need to do, as a result."

Finally, at the close of the day, Jesus joins the two disciples around a table. He breaks bread and, in doing so, breaks open the mystery of his presence. He was "made known to them in the breaking of the bread." It may be stretching the point to suggest that this was a communion service. However, it certainly is not stretching anything to say that, as we gather around our communion tables, we expect that in the mystery of the sacrament Jesus will make himself known to us. Through bread and wine he is present.

This, of course, is not the end of the story. Those two disciples didn't just carry on down the road to Emmaus, the road to nowhere. Instead, because of what had happened, they were able to go back to the city, back to what they were running from. Few of us want to go back to the painful situations we have left. Dr. Norman De Puis suggests that what Jesus did for these two men was to redeem their past. He took their memories of brokenness and rewrote them in such a way that fear and guilt were taken away. He helped them recognize that their pain was not for nothing: there was purpose in it.

When the two men returned to the city, they could hardly wait to tell their story to their friends. Like them, and like my friend in the Twelve Step Program, we will want to do the same.

Emmaus is whatever we do or wherever we go to make ourselves forget that the world holds nothing sacred, says Frederick Buechner. But the Christian, travelling this road, meets the One who listens and who makes sense out of the pain. He is the One who breaks the bread and in this mystery restores the sacred, redeems the past, and makes it possible to go home again.

*Can you recall some "Friday" moment of your life,
from which you wanted to get away?*

*Ask God to be with you, transforming you
through that memory.*

❧  ☙

*O Lord, Christ Jesus,
who gave new life to disciples in despair:
when I am pursued by worldly pain and sorrow,
walk with me, talk with me, reveal your purpose for me,
that I may be glad in the knowledge of your grace:
in your name, I ask.
Amen.*

# 4

# Dealing with Our Demons

☙ ❧

*There was in their synagogue a man with an unclean spirit, and he cried out, "What have you to do with us, Jesus of Nazareth? Have you come to destroy us? I know who you are, the Holy One of God." But Jesus rebuked him, saying, "Be silent, and come out of him!"*

— Mark 1:23–25

I remember having lunch with a man who told me of the deep hurt caused by his recent separation from his wife. His life had dramatically changed. "What disturbs me most," he said, "are these voices that I've never heard before. They come when I least expect them — in what friends say, in a dream, in things I read. I sometimes wonder if they come from God. These voices tell me that I don't matter, that I'm only half a person, that no one cares how I feel, that things will never change. I feel that I'm in a kind of a penalty box and I will be here for a long time."

In times of crisis and pain, most of us hear these voices that drag us down. They are the demons that possess us, the unclean spirits of a story told in the first chapter of Mark's gospel. In the middle of the sermon at the synagogue in Capernaum, a man suddenly jumps up and interrupts the preacher. "What have you to do with us, Jesus of Nazareth? Have you come to destroy us? I know who you are, the Holy One of God." This man is not out of his mind. He knows where he is. He knows the preacher, and he knows what the preacher is saying. But, something is wrong. Mark's diagnosis is possession by an evil spirit.

Jesus immediately recognizes a tormented human being who needs healing and care. Jesus sees past the violent verbal attack, senses the man's fear, pain, and confusion, and understands that they come not from the man himself but from somewhere else. Jesus clearly sees evil as a spiritual force that, if permitted or encouraged, can demean and even destroy life. He sees a dark force resident in the personality of this unfortunate man, battling against the rest of him. Jesus' response is, "Be silent, and come out of him!"

This story emphasizes a recurring theme in Mark's gospel: Jesus continually confronts evil forces and defeats them.

Most of us these days are uncomfortable with the subject of evil. We have been so used to blaming sickness or parental neglect or the environment for the ills that befall people, that we find it difficult to identify evil as a force in its own right. During most of the twentieth century, we have been taught that evil can be institutionalized, that you can send it either to a hospital or a prison and all will be well. But as we enter a new century, we are confronted with cases that overthrow our assumptions. In the murders of children by other children, even in the safe havens of their schools, and in the faces of rapists and murderers, we see something very dark that we cannot explain. This is what Jesus saw that day in the synagogue. Behind the pain and fear of this distraught man, he saw an evil force that had taken over the man.

The gospel story tells us something about our own demons — those things that afflict us, depress us, and cause us grief. How often do our minds wander back to a past hurt, and a tide of guilt or regret rolls over us? How often do we wake up at four o'clock in the morning, and some small negative thing takes over our minds and puts an end to our sleep? How often, like the man recently separated from his wife, do we feel belittled and put down? But the demons lie.

Too often in the media we read heart-wrenching accounts of the abuse of children, frequently at the hands of their parents. A few years ago I read a report about a child in New England whose parents had kept her locked in a closet for much of her early life. Deprived of socialization and without any education, the young girl knew only abuse and neglect. Finally, at the age of fifteen, she was discovered and rescued. After much intensive therapy in a new environment, where she began to trust the love of a new family, she slowly found some sense of self-value. At the trial of her parents, the judge asked her if she had anything to say. Shaking and sobbing, she banged the table with her fist and, looking at her parents, cried out, "I am a some-body. You lied to me!"

When we battle against our own demons — jealousy, lust, addiction, guilt, depression — we often hear voices that put us down and discourage us. We need to know that these voices lie. God has the truth about us: the truth of our dignity, our worth, and our value in his sight.

I believe that we conquer the voices of fear, negativity, and despair by listening to other voices. The Bible can help us here. A woman once told me that she would often wake up in the middle of the night, her head filled with heavy thoughts. She said, "I found if I left my Bible open at Psalm 23 and my glasses on top of it, I could counter my loneliness with the voice that said, 'The Lord is my shepherd ... he leads me beside still waters ... I fear no evil; for you are with me.'"

Someone should write a little book of things that God wants to say to us at three o'clock in the morning: "Do not be afraid, I am with you. I hold you in the palm of my hand." "The Lord is full of compassion and mercy." "Do not be anxious. Consider the birds of the air. Your father feeds them. Are you not more valuable than birds?" "I will not leave you alone, I will come to you." These are the voices that we need to hear — voices that call us to wholeness, holiness, and hope.

The good news in the story that St. Mark tells is that Jesus healed the man. The demon left him and he was whole again. The Lord's spirit of goodness is stronger than any demon — and it is God's will for us.

In one of the great galleries in Europe hangs a picture of Faust and the devil playing chess. They are playing for Faust's soul. The devil has won and Faust is checkmated. The devil's face is flushed with victorious glee, and Faust's is full of despair. There is a story that people by the thousands used to come and look at this work and say, "Yes, that's the way it is. We're locked in, and there's nothing we can do. Life is like that. We always lose." One day a great chess master came to the gallery and stood for hours staring at the painting. Suddenly he cried out, "It's a lie, it's a lie! The game is not over. Look! The king and the knight still have moves left." Life is not a penalty box. The demons of our lives do not have the final word.

For us, the good news is that the game is never lost. Our Lord Jesus Christ has won the great victory over all the demons. And by his love and forgiveness, we are included in the triumph. No evil force, not even death itself, can destroy us.

*Can you recall a demon in your life,*
*a persistently*
*painful thought or feeling?*

*Hear the voice of Jesus commanding,*
*"Be silent. Come out."*

⁂

*O Lord, Christ Jesus,*
*who healed the sick and drove away the demons:*
*when evil thoughts and madness threaten to devour me,*
*show me your holy light shining in the darkness,*
*cleansing and healing, restoring my soul;*
*my Saviour and my God.*
*Amen.*

# 5

# When It's Hard to Forgive and Forget

*Then Joseph said to his brothers, "Come closer to me." And they came closer. He said, "I am your brother, Joseph, whom you sold into Egypt. And now do not be distressed, or angry with yourselves, because you sold me here; for God sent me before you to preserve life."*

— Genesis 45:4–5

One of the hardest things we ever have to do is to forgive and forget. When we are hurt — abandoned, rejected, criticized, misunderstood, or abused — a relationship is damaged or broken. Forgiveness is meant to be the instrument of reconciliation and peace.

Frankly, forgiveness can tire you out. Say you have a lunch date with a friend that you go to a lot of trouble to keep. You leave work early enough to be there on time. You circle the block three times to find a parking spot. Then in the restaurant you wait and wait and wait. Finally, when it's clear that you've been stood up, you eat your salad, pay the bill, and leave. That evening your friend phones to explain that she'd left her appointment book at home and forgotten your lunch date. "Can we do it again?" Of course, you say "yes." The day arrives and the same thing happens all over again.

Forgiving someone once is one thing. But will you do it again? Human nature often does not work this way. Most of us are willing to be burnt once, a lot of us twice, but not any more. As Barbara Brown Taylor says, "It's as if we have these little calculators in our heads keeping track of how much we are putting into relationships versus how much we are getting out" (*The Seeds of Heaven*).

Philip Yancey, in an article entitled "The Terrible Logic of Unfogiveness," talks about the terrible price the world pays for "chronic, logical unforgiveness." Citing wars in the former Yugoslavia, he writes, "The Serbs, of course, are everybody's whipping boy. What has happened in Bosnia and Kosovo is squalor and barbarism, the filthy work of liars and cynics, manipulating tribal prejudices and old blood feuds. But caught up in our righteous revulsion over all of these things, we might forget one fact. The people of Yugoslavia are simply following the terrible logic of unforgiveness" (*Christianity Today*).

The story of logical unforgiveness is by no means limited to the Balkans. Most of us could add a chapter of our own, from our experience of the struggle between revenge and resolution.

And yet sometimes there is a breakthrough. In South Africa, racism was institutionalized for decades in the system of apartheid, which physically separated the black majority from the white minority and spent only one-tenth as much money educating a black child as educating a white child. The cycle of vengeance and violence grew until, with the help of two clear-sighted visionaries, people cut through it. They were both Anglican Christians: Archbishop Desmond Tutu and former President Nelson Mandela. The program of uncovering uncomfortable truths and seeking reconciliation that they established has been amazingly successful in substituting forgiveness for vengeance.

In Northern Ireland, the road remains rocky. But there too efforts to end to decades of vengeful unforgiveness are showing some success. Here in Canada, we face a similar challenge in undoing the damage done by years of racist discrimination against native peoples. Their anger, their militancy, their court claims against governments and churches are all entirely understandable, and so are the responses of the white majority when they say, "But it's not our fault." From the midst of all the confusion and resentment, we can hear a call to forgiveness.

The issue is not whether or not we should forgive. Most of us know we should. But to say it is one thing; to do it is quite another. The issue for most of us is how to forgive, and perhaps we also need to know why.

The Old Testament story of Joseph may set us thinking. When Joseph receives the coat of many of colours, the rest of Jacob's sons are jealous of their father's favour. So his own family, who should have loved him, sell him into slavery. Joseph, once the privileged boy with the silver spoon in his mouth, becomes a victim of abuse and is taken away to a strange land. But Joseph does not play the victim. Although he finds himself to be a slave, he is a slave in a good household. People recognize his talents and appreciate him. He learns to be responsible. Gone is the brash, arrogant brat that he used to be. Joseph would say that, in his slavery, he met God.

Then one day his past comes back. There, in front of him, stand his brothers, but this time they are begging. There is famine in Israel, and they have come to buy food in Egypt. Since Joseph is in charge, they are sent to him. They don't recognize him, but he recognizes them. He goes off alone and cries, growing angry as the memories of hurt flood back. At first, he sends them away empty-handed, but later he overhears them saying that they believe their current troubles are punishment for selling a brother into slavery long ago.

Later still, the story carries on: "Joseph could no longer control himself and he said to his brothers, 'Come closer to me. I am your brother, Joseph, whom you sold into Egypt. And now do not be distressed, or angry with yourselves, because you sold me here; for God sent me before you to preserve life....' And he kissed all his brothers and wept upon them." Then, loading them with food for the homeward journey, he begs them to return bringing their father, their families, and all their possessions to live secure in Egypt's plenty until the famine in Canaan is past.

Joseph seized the opportunity for something better than revenge. He forgave his family the wrong that they had done him. How many of us need to do the same? The media stories of abuse within families are only the tip of the iceberg — the spectacular ones that hit the headlines. How many petty meannesses do we suffer in our families and harbour in our hearts? Beyond the family we think of friends who have hurt us, colleagues at school and work, neighbours, casual acquaintances.

But Joseph also forgave an enemy inside himself — that part of him that had been deeply hurt and become bitter, angry, and alone. When people say, "He's his own worst enemy," they are referring to the way we are hard on ourselves and deprecate ourselves. Nothing hurts us more than the bitterness and anger that we harbour.

But where do we find the energy to forgive? Joseph was able to forgive his brothers because, as he said, "It was not you who sent me here, but God." He saw the hurt in a wider context of God's love.

A great saint of the twentieth century was German pastor Dietrich Bonhoeffer. He was one of a minority of pastors and laypeople who separated from the main body of the German Lutheran church when it officially backed a version of Hitler's Nazi ideology, and later he was executed for his part in a conspiracy to assassinate Hitler. In *Letters and Papers from Prison* written from a Nazi prison cell, Bonhoeffer insisted that being saved doesn't mean "redemption from cares, distress, fears, and longings, from sin and death, in a better world beyond the grave." Instead, like Christ, the Christian "must drink the earthly cup to the dregs, and only in doing so is the crucified and risen Lord with him, and he crucified and risen with Christ.... Christ takes hold of a man at the centre of his life." The energy to forgive comes from recognizing that Christ is with us in the hard work of forgiveness, because it is his work too.

When a teenager was shot dead at a school in Alberta not long ago, his father, an Anglican priest, was able afterward to forgive the offender. One summer I was called back from my holidays because a parishioner had been involved in a deadly accident. Coming out of a party early Sunday morning after drinking heavily, he drove the wrong way on a one-way street. Two motorcyclists hit his car. Both died. When I met with him and his parents the next day, he was a very sober, distraught young man, facing serious charges and burdened with profound guilt. On the morning of the funeral of one of the victims, the mother of the boy to be buried phoned. She said, "We've just come from Holy Communion. Please tell your son that we forgive him." Although none of those people would ever be the same after the tragedy, healing for all of them had begun through these gracious acts of forgiveness.

Where did they find what it took to forgive? As Christians they knew that their Lord, dying on the cross, forgave the people who had caused him to be there. Who were those people? People like you and me. In fact, those people include you and me. And we have been forgiven! Nothing we can do is so terrible that the loving God cannot forgive us. Knowing that we are forgiven gives us the energy and strength to forgive ourselves for our bitterness and anger, and from there the next step follows naturally: forgiving those who offend us or cause us harm. Forgiveness frees us from the prison of the past — the terrible logic of unforgiveness — and allows us to get on with our lives.

*Recall experiences you have had of forgiving*
*and being forgiven.*

*What opportunities for forgiving and being forgiven*
*are open to you now?*

&2&

*O Lord, Christ Jesus,*
*who endured bitter cruelty and death, yet forgave:*
*give me the courage to forgive myself,*
*and the grace to forgive others,*
*that you may live in me,*
*and I in you.*
*Amen.*

# 6

# A Magnificent Defeat

*Jacob was left alone; and a man wrestled with him until daybreak.*

— Genesis 32:24

A great criticism made about churchgoers is that our lifestyle and values differ little from people who share our culture but seem to care little for spiritual things. At a reception following a wedding, a man introduced himself to me as a "used-to-be Anglican" and, for some reason, felt the need to justify his status. "I guess I'm as good as the next guy," he said. "A partner of mine goes to church every Sunday. I don't see much difference between the way he lives and the way I live. I guess I'll be okay."

It's true, being a Christian doesn't guarantee that people will be caring and compassionate. It doesn't even mean that they won't do terrible things. History tells us about the wars fought over religion between Protestants and Roman Catholics, and even today a relic of that struggle is found in Northern Ireland. The wars in the former Yugoslavia have a religious component: Orthodox Serbs against Roman Catholic Croats and Albanian Muslims. How can people go to church and then ethnically cleanse each other?

I recently read an article in an American magazine noting that, in Alabama, people have a high rate of belief in evangelical religion. "They believe not only in God but in the divinity of Christ and inspiration of scripture. It is puzzling therefore," said the article, "that Alabama has some of the highest rates of illegitimacy, divorce, abortion, and violent crime." Over the years Christians have defended slavery, fought to keep women in a position inferior to men, and persecuted gay people. In present-day Canada we are acutely aware of the abuses that were perpetrated on aboriginal children in Christian residential schools, and we know that Christians are involved in the political attack on the poor.

Of course, these crimes and injustices are the work not only of Christians, but surely Christians ought to set examples of kindness, justice, compassion, and understanding. So the question for us is, How can Christianity be integrated into our whole being so, that our lives are transformed and made Christ-like?

In the Old Testament, Jacob, the grandson of Abraham, was brighter and more creative than his older brother Esau. Realizing that Esau was in line for the full inheritance upon their father's death, Jacob devised a scheme to cheat his brother and get their father's blessing. When Esau found out and threatened to kill him, Jacob had to flee. One night he was alone, camped on a hillside to the north. He lay down with a stone for a pillow and dreamed not the nightmare of the guilty, but a dream of incredible and mystical beauty. He saw a ladder reaching up to heaven with angels ascending and descending. God was there too, promising that Jacob would be the father of a great nation. Jacob woke up with a new and profound sense of God's reality and his presence. "Surely the Lord is in this place — and I did not know it," he said. "How awesome is this place! This is none other than the house of God, and this is the gate of heaven." All of this was a wonderful affirmation for a man who was on the run for cheating his brother. It seemed to indicate to Jacob that God too was on his side.

Most of us at some time in life have some kind of experience of God's presence. It may happen in church. Some people tell me that, just by walking into a certain church building, they sense God's spirit. Others speak of a more personal time, a mystical experience that is hard to put into words. It may happen among close friends or in the presence of nature. Often these experiences come out of the blue and the result is affirmation. "I'm not alone. Someone loves me." There is a sense of the transcendent, of being part of something or someone greater than oneself.

But sometimes there is also a sense of pride in our spiritual accomplishments. It might show in the firm belief that many people have in prayer as a cure for physical illness. In fact, there is a lot of evidence that prayer does help to cure illnesses — one's own and other people's. It can lower blood pressure and anxiety, alleviate fear and depression, and lead to better health.

But if our only reason for believing in God is that it makes us feel good, something very important is missing. Jesus was critical of people who made a lot of their religion or took it up for selfish reasons, like the Pharisee who thanked God that he was not like other people, and who fasted twice a week and tithed regularly. Jesus even said that a person who claimed to love God but hated his brother was a liar! Those would have been hard words for Jacob to hear. The question is, How do we connect our religious belief and experience with our moral behaviour? How do we follow our Lord's example and become compassionate healers of the world's ills?

Jacob's experience on that stone pillow frankly was not enough. Yes, he felt God's presence. Yes, he was affirmed. Yes, he felt better. Probably his blood pressure dropped to normal rates. But in the story his lifestyle didn't change very much. He certainly didn't try to undo the injustice done to his brother; in fact, he was emotionally abusive to one of his wives and got embroiled in endless disputes with his father-in-law. The experience of the mystical dream at Bethel was simply something added to his life, not something that transformed or changed it.

Every one of us needs to ask this question: Is my religious experience something piled on top of all my other experiences, or does it really change, disturb, and heal the deeper areas of my life?

Jacob needed another kind of experience with God, and he got it. He felt called to return home, but he dreaded the meeting with his brother that would force him to face his past. He took the precaution of sending gifts to appease Esau. The night he spent alone before the meeting was a terrible night. The story tells of someone coming to him and wrestling with him. There was a struggle until dawn, until suddenly the mysterious assailant struck him on the hip and put it out of joint. When the struggle was over, Jacob realized that this too was an experience of God. He had wrestled with God and lost.

Suddenly everything changed for Jacob. His brother appeared and, far from being angry, fell on his neck and kissed him, and they both wept. "To see your face," said Jacob, "is like seeing the face of God.... God has dealt graciously with me." In losing the battle, Jacob had been transformed. Gone was the arrogance; gone was the pride. There was reconciliation and a new beginning. Frederick Buechner calls it the Magnificent Defeat.

Often it is the defeats that heal us. Healing is a different matter from physical curing. When a paralyzed man was lowered through a hole in the roof, so that Jesus could cure him, Jesus told him that his sins were forgiven, and then he was cured. Jacob must have felt something like that. Sometimes there is no physical cure for an illness, yet a dying person still testifies to being healed — delivered from anxiety and selfish concerns, healed in mind and soul and spirit.

I remember a man telling me about the time that his ten-year-old daughter was diagnosed with leukemia. He was a very successful man and also a man of faith, an elder in his church. This crisis became for him as much a spiritual crisis as a medical and family crisis. His daughter did survive, but the man's faith was shaken. "For two years," he said, "I fought with God.

I was angry and confused. My life was in pieces. Then slowly a new God started to emerge — a God that loved me personally as I was, who didn't want my strength or my successes. He wanted rather to meet me in my weakness and in order that he might make me strong his way." A magnificent defeat.

Like Jacob, we need not only a spiritual experience that affirms and excites and lifts us up, but also one that heals and transforms us deep within. This often happens through a time of struggle — a time when we don't run away from issues but deal with them and meet God in the struggle.

Jesus' work seemed to end in utter failure and utter defeat. Hanging on the cross, helpless and scorned, he cried out to the God he felt had deserted him, and then he died. But this wasn't the end of the story. Three days later his followers were seeing him alive and hailing God's great victory. What a magnificent defeat the crucifixion is!

The defeat of our pride, our arrogance, and our self-interest is magnificent because humility, integrity, compassion — all the good things of God — win. Our lives are transformed, and this is the beginning of the transformation of all those terrible evils and injustices that surround us. Transformed ourselves, we become God's agents through whom God transforms and redeems a suffering world.

*Has there been an experience of*
*apparent humiliation and defeat in your life?*

*Ask God to show you how you grew in grace as a result.*

⋦ ⋧

*O Lord, Christ Jesus,*
*who suffered and died, yet lives and reigns:*
*in losing give me hope, in winning give me gratitude,*
*that your grace may transform all my living*
*and your love infuse all my deeds;*
*in your name, I ask.*
*Amen.*

# 7

# Finding God in the Wilderness

*The wilderness and the dry land will be glad, the desert shall rejoice and blossom.*

— Isaiah 35

I have noticed from reading Christmas letters that many of our friends have been spending time in the wilderness — camping, hiking, climbing, and having a lot of fun. We North Americans have had an interesting relationship with our wilderness. It was only about a hundred years ago that most of our continent was natural land. It was home to the First Nations people, who saw wilderness as sacred. The land, the cycle of the seasons, even the weather — all were sacred. But for the first European settlers, wilderness was an enemy to be conquered. People got lost in the wilderness and died. Survival depended upon driving the wilderness back and protecting oneself against it. Many of us still have some of this attitude in our blood.

However, in the last few decades we've been hearing a different story about wilderness. Instead of fearing it, many of us are fascinated by it and take refuge in it. We have once again recognized that health — in fact, our very survival — depends upon the health of the nature. Wilderness travel has become big business. Like the First Nations and the Celts — whose spiritual traditions have grown so popular of late — we have found that there are things about being human that we can best discover in the shadow of a pine tree beside the rush of a white water stream.

It's been suggested that the wilderness holds answers to questions we have not yet learned to ask." After a few days in the wilderness, we find that our lives deepen and, though otherwise unaccustomed to doing so, we may use the name of God. "But," says Eugene Peterson, "there's also something frightening about the wilderness. There is this tension between the beauty and the danger, and for that reason it is a place where we can never be totally in control" (*Leap Over a Wall*).

Many native North American cultures observed the tradition of the vision quest. A young person was initiated into adulthood by being led out into the wilderness to a certain sacred spot and left alone there for some days to seek a vision. The seeking took the form of prayer and meditation, and the vision gave deep insight into oneself and the world around. Nowadays, many people attend Outward Bound courses. These courses put participants into wilderness situations that demand the most of them — physically, mentally, emotionally, and spiritually. Some include a version of the vision quest, with the person spending some days alone in the wilderness. Most participants say that they return from such courses with a different and deeper understanding of themselves, relationships, other people, and the world at large. Many of the young people who attend summer camps report similar deep experiences.

The common thread here is that wilderness offers challenges simply because we are not ourselves totally in control. But responding to the challenges increases awareness of self and others and nature itself. At the deepest level, the encounter with wilderness increases awareness of the presence of God, who is in all these experiences.

The Bible has nearly three hundred references to wilderness; in many of these texts, wilderness is the place where people have little control over their lives. When Adam and Eve rebelled against God, they were evicted from the beautiful garden to the wilderness east of Eden. When the children of Israel left Egypt, they wandered in the wilderness for forty years. When John the Baptist began to preach, he called people into the wilderness to repent. When Jesus began his ministry, he withdrew to the wilderness where he was tempted by Satan. In all these examples, wilderness deprives people of control over their lives, leaving them vulnerable and sometimes in danger.

For the prophet Isaiah, wilderness is a metaphor for human emptiness and isolation. Isaiah writes as if he himself knew very well the reality of the human wilderness — its beauty, danger, loneliness, and fear. How, he asks, are we to survive it? But as he stands in the place of isolation and loneliness, he has a vision of a better reality: "The wilderness and the dry land shall be glad, the desert shall rejoice and blossom." In the wilderness Isaiah sees a miracle of hope because God is active there, with dramatic consequences. "Say to those who are of a fearful heart, ... 'Be strong, do not fear! ... Here is your God.'... Then the eyes of the blind shall be opened, and the ears of the deaf unstopped; then the lame shall leap like a deer, and the tongue of the speechless sing for joy.... Sorrow and sighing shall flee away."

Ironically, we are so busy surviving, so busy trying to stay in control, that we fail to notice God waiting to meet us in the wilderness. Perhaps we need to take time out in the wilderness of nature, when we can, to encounter God. This is the apparently positive side of wilderness that our contemporaries have rediscovered. However, there is another less obvious kind of wilderness encounter: the wilderness moments of life — times when we are confused, uncertain, despairing, and full of fear — times when we lose control. You lose your job. A loved one dies. You are very sick. A relationship has broken down. These too are times when God is waiting to meet us. Those who can let go of the need to control everything, admit their fear and helplessness, and say, "I can't do this thing called life alone," find that the wilderness blossoms into rejoicing. The wilderness is where God is found.

I knew a woman named Anne who found that it is the need for control, not the wilderness, that separates us from the love of God. She was in her late forties and suffering from terminal cancer. Her husband had died from the same disease about four years before. Never a strongly religious person, she discovered something quite remarkable in her wilderness of pain. "The strange irony of this journey," she said, "is that God has become so close, not as a means for a miracle but just his presence. In all of this, I feel profoundly loved. I know that I'm okay and I will be okay."

Moses and the children of Israel, wandering in the wilderness of Sinai, were hungry and thirsty, but one morning they found the ground covered with manna; and when Moses struck a rock, the water flowed forth. Isaiah wept over the wilderness that had once been the holy city of Jerusalem, but in it he saw new life springing up in the form of flowers that promised hope and transformation. When people heeded the call of John the Baptist to come out into the wilderness and repent, they found themselves filled with new hope. Mary, the mother of Jesus, bewildered by the confusion of pregnancy out of wedlock, heard the voice of the angel saying, "Greetings, favoured one! The Lord is with you." And she replied, "Here am I, the servant of the Lord; let it be with me according to your word."

Our Lord himself spent troubled times in the wilderness. Tempted there by Satan, he was filled with the power of the Spirit and returned to Galilee to begin his ministry of teaching and healing. At the end of his ministry, hanging on the cross, he suffered ultimate loss of control. But even the terrifying wilderness experience of being utterly abandoned, in pain, and near death was transformed. It led to a glorious resurrection that offers us the certain hope that, when we are most alone, most in fear and danger, and least in control, the loving God is with us, holding us and raising us up.

In fact, we are most likely to experience the love, mercy, and power of God at these weak moments in our lives. As Eugene Peterson writes in *Leap Over a Wall*, "When we find ourselves in the wilderness we do well to be frightened. We also do well to be alert. In the wilderness we're plunged into an awareness of danger and death but at the same time, if we let ourselves be, we are plunged into an awareness of the great mystery of God and the extraordinary preciousness of life."

*Can you recall a time when you have felt alone
and afraid: perhaps even now?*

*Let the presence of God surround you
and transform you.*

*O God, our creator,
who made all things and lives in all things:
enliven my senses, awaken my spirit,
that in my distress I may find you
waiting in the wilderness,
to nourish my hope
and my life.
Amen.*

# 8

# Finding a Story
# to Live By

*So God created humankind in his own image. In the image*
*of God he created them; male and female he created them.*

— Genesis 1:27

Probably the most important book in my library is a book of
daily lectionary readings from the Bible. It is a very handy book
because it contains two readings and a psalm for each weekday
of the Christian year. In it I have a bookmark, which is actually
an old letter that I grabbed one day from a pile of paper. It was
just the right size, and I kept moving it forward to mark my
place, far more interested in my book than the bookmark.

Then one day I opened the letter and read it. It was written
about ten years ago to my wife and me by a teacher in western
Canada. Two of her friends were on stress leave from teaching,

another had separated and divorced, and the wife of a colleague had taken her own life. She closed the letter with the words, "It's a crazy world; how can we ever understand it?" I guess what really struck me was her matter-of-fact style, as if all this bad news should come as no surprise — that's the way life is.

Of all the longings in our lives, none is more pressing than the need to make sense of the chaos and confusion of life. Bruce Larson tells the story of his Aunt Mary, who every Christmas would send as her gift a giant jigsaw puzzle. Starting on Christmas night, the family would spread all the pieces out on a card table and begin. The fun lasted throughout the holidays. One Christmas when the gift arrived as usual, the family took a good look at the picture on the box and started to work; but after fifteen minutes of frustration, they realized that the picture and puzzle didn't match. After a couple of phone calls, the mystery was solved: Aunt Mary had switched the top of the puzzle with one she had sent to her other nephews. The following year they got the puzzle without any picture at all. Try as they could to imagine what the picture might have been, they found it impossible. They had all the right pieces, but no picture to follow.

Many of us remember a time when there was a picture to guide us in fitting together the pieces of our lives and making sense of them and of the world around us. But at the dawn of the twenty-first century, we have lost it. The poet Edna St. Vincent Millay wrote,

Upon this gifted age in its dark hour
Rains from the sky a meteoric shower

Of facts that lie unquestioned, uncombined.
Wisdom enough to leech us of our will — daily spun.
But there exists no loom to weave it into fabric.

In our world we are deluged daily by information that comes "unquestioned, uncombined," with no indication of which bits fit where and what their value or importance is. There is no story, no great narrative — no frame of reference — by which we can assemble them, make sense, and find meaning.

In his 1999 CBC Massey Lectures, Robert Fulford notes that there was a time when the Bible was the defining narrative of the Western world. It showed how the pieces of our culture and our lives fitted to create a picture that could be understood. But this narrative has been abandoned by the majority. We now live in a world of many pictures and many identities. We call it pluralism. The great dream was that, with so much choice, no one would be left out.

We now live in a world where people must choose the story they live by. No longer does the culture provide a dominant, defining story. Culture, science, business, and government produce the pieces of the puzzle, but not the picture that guides us in placing the pieces and making sense of them. Instead, we are left to choose our own picture and to try making the pieces fit into it. We are on our own to find meaning and purpose.

Those of us who persist in the Christian faith and want our children to share it with us know that the Bible offers the guidance we need. Out of necessity, we must become more and more a Bible-centred people because we need the Bible's defining narrative to lead us in understanding truth and to direct us in leading our lives. I want to suggest three lifestyle implications of choosing this sacred narrative.

First, in choosing any narrative, we have to trust it. This does not mean that we have no questions or doubts but, if the story is to work in our lives, we must be able to trust its integrity. Approaching scripture only with suspicion — "Oh, you can't believe that! In six days? Science doesn't support that" or "Poor Eve, obviously the victim of male exploitation" — doesn't get us very far. Right at the beginning of the Bible, the Book of Genesis makes one great truth clear: all created things are essentially good. "God saw everything he had made, and indeed it was very good." The story says that life did not happen by chance or by random accident. It was planned, and in the planning it was infused with atoms of divinity that link it with its Creator. Believing this has implications for the way we live. Our personal selves are valuable, sacred, and worthy. Other people are also valuable, sacred, and worthy. So is the whole earth and all that lives on it.

And so we must ask questions about the brave new world that some conceive. Should we permit termination of the lives of children born with severe disabilities? Should we support genetic engineering that claims to eliminate certain diseases and disabilities, or that even claims to produce superior people? Should we permit painful tests to be used on animals? Should we support a system that treats people as if they were born to serve the economy and not the other way around?

Should we allow the gap between rich and poor to continue to widen? Should we continue to exploit the world's non-renewable natural resources, or allow pollution to continue, or continue to create mountains of waste that no one can satisfactorily dispose of? These questions and many more like them arise as a consequence of accepting a defining narrative that leads us to understand that we and all things on earth are sacred.

The second implication of choosing the Bible as our narrative is that our personal identity goes deeper than ethnicity, race, gender, or sexuality. In each of us there is something more original than any of those marks of identity. In St. Luke's gospel, the account of Jesus' genealogy does not stop at Abraham. It goes back to Adam and Eve. Jesus was more than just an ethnic Jew. Our roots also go right back to Eden, where we find our common identity. When you walk down the street of a Canadian city and see a young man whose father may have been an Inuit hunter, or a girl who may have recently arrived from a refugee camp in the Sudan, you are seeing a brother or sister, a child of our common mother, Eve.

The third implication of the Bible as defining narrative is that the sacredness of all things derives from God. We are not sacred like ancient kings because of who our parents were. Nor are we sacred because of our wealth: the beggar on the street is as sacred as the successful entrepreneur. Not even our own accomplishments make us sacred: great artists, doctors, and engineers share sacred human life with the most ordinary of folk. And we are learning that our failure to regard all life as sacred

— the life of plants and animals, and the life of planet Earth — has brought us to the brink of ecological disaster. We are all pieces in the sacred picture created by the loving God.

It occurs to me that it is hard to find meaning in the sad story told by my letter bookmark, and still harder to know how to respond to it without the spirit and story of the book it marks. My bookmark, therefore, with all its pain and questions, is in the right place.

*Recall an episode in the Bible that you especially like,*
*and take time to read it again.*

*How does this story help to give meaning*
*and purpose to your life?*

❧ ❧

*O God, our creator,*
*a Trinity in unity, three persons in one God:*
*when chaos and disorder threaten to dissolve my life,*
*let me see your goodness and order in creation,*
*in animals and plants, in humankind,*
*in sun and sky, in land and water,*
*embracing all, uniting all;*
*in your name, I ask.*
*Amen.*

# 9

# Do You Have to Walk on Water to Be a Christian?

*By this time the boat, battered by the waves, was far from the land, for the wind was against them. And early in the morning Jesus came walking toward them on the sea. But when the disciples saw him walking on the sea, they were terrified, saying, "It is a ghost!" And they cried out in fear. But immediately Jesus spoke to them and said, "Take heart, it is I; do not be afraid."*

— Matthew 14:24–27

Some time ago, a young man came to my office to talk about his developing faith. He had been baptized and confirmed just the year before and was new at being a Christian. A very serious

person, he was having some difficulty. "It isn't easy," he said, "to be a real Christian. I just read the Sermon on the Mount. How can I ever live up to that? How can I forgive all the time, love my enemies all the time, turn the other cheek? I have a lot of questions. Do you really have to walk on water to be a Christian?"

Walking on water is a symbol of doing the impossible. All of us know how hard it is at times to be a follower of Jesus Christ, and we all ask, Do you really have to walk on water to be a Christian? Life presents us with many impossible situations. How do parents respond to the child who disappoints their every hope? Or how does the child respond to parents whose harsh and unreasonable demands never stop? What do we do when our work seems to require that we abandon the care for others that Christian morality requires: for example, in firing a person who has worked well and has a family to feed, or in taking advantage of a situation that may harm a competitor? Should we buy products made by exploited labour or by processes that harm the environment?

What seems like the Christian response to situations like these may cost us a great deal. Are we really expected to pay that much — in patient self-sacrificing kindness, in risking security or money, in putting ourselves at a disadvantage? Time and again we find ourselves called on to make impossible decisions — at sea, far from the safety of land, and battered by the waves.

This story is about Peter, who sees Jesus walking on the water and says, "Lord, if it is you, command me to come to you

on the water." He climbs out of the boat and starts walking toward Jesus, but then, noticing the strong wind, he becomes frightened and begins to sink. "Lord, save me," he cries. Jesus reaches out his hand, catches him, and helps him into the boat. And then he asks Peter, "You of little faith, why did you doubt?" It seems that Peter failed a test of faith. This is what the young man felt who came to see me. It is what many of us feel.

However, there is a word of hope here for us all. Jesus reached out and saved Peter! And he called on all of them to take heart and not be afraid because he, Jesus, was there with them in the storm. This should assure us that Jesus is with us too, in all the storms of life. In fact, we are every bit as likely to meet Jesus in the difficult moments as in the peace and calm of a warm summer evening by the lake, or at a service in church, or in our own quiet prayer time.

The great twentieth-century martyr Dietrich Bonhoeffer said that we are apt to think redemption means "redemption from cares, distress, fears, and longings, from sin and death, in a better world beyond the grave. But is this really the essential character of the proclamation of Christ in the gospels and by Paul? I should say not.... The Christian hope of resurrection ... sends a man back to his life on earth in a wholly new way.... The Christian must drink the earthly cup to the dregs, and only in his doing so is the crucified and risen Lord with him.... Christ takes hold of a man at the centre of his life" (*Letters and Papers from Prison*).

St. Peter takes the plunge — and the Lord is there with him. Even when Peter's heart fails him, the Lord reaches out his hand and takes hold of him. The gentle rebuke, "You of little faith, why did you doubt?" is actually an assurance that Peter will remember next time. So Peter didn't fail in faith; he found out what faith really is: discovering Christ in the crisis.

Like Peter, we too have to take risks. The surfer Phil Edwards has written, "There is a need in all of us for controlled danger; that is, a need of an activity that puts us on the edge of life. There are too many of us going through life without any vibrant kick to life. I call them the legions of the unjazzed." He says that surfing needs two things. "First, you need to go out where the deep water is and find the big waves. Second, once on board you need to lean into the wave." We too must go out into deep water and lean into life, lean into work, lean into relationships. Only when we do this will we experience the loving hands reaching out and lifting us up. It takes courage. But we can hear those words, "Take heart, it is I; do not be afraid."

Do we really have to walk on water to be a Christian? Do we really have to attempt the impossible? This is the wrong question. Christ meets us in the situations that seem most impossible, and with him all things are possible.

*Is there some constructive thing*
*you always wanted to do but feared to do?*
*Imagine yourself taking that risk,*
*and Jesus supporting you.*

*O Lord, Christ Jesus,*
*who saved the disciple who trusted in you:*
*remind me, when I fear to venture in your name,*
*that you are by my side, your hand in mine*
*to lift me up, to bear me on the water,*
*to bring me through the storm;*
*in your name, I ask.*
*Amen.*

# 10

# The Spiritual Habits of Highly Effective People

⚜ ⚜

*You are the salt of the earth; but if the salt has lost its taste, how can its saltiness be restored? It is no longer good for anything, but is thrown out and trampled under foot.*

— Matthew 5:13

Stephen Covey's famous bestseller, *Seven Habits of Highly Effective People*, came out just at the beginning of a very painful recession. People in business were wondering what was happening to them, and the title promised some solace. At first look, it may have appeared to be just another self-help manual offering seven easy steps to survival, but the book is not about easy fixes. Instead, it shows that effectiveness is a matter of character. What makes you effective is not what you do, but who you are as a person.

The Sermon on the Mount in St. Matthew's gospel is also about the kind of people we have to be in order to be effective. Jesus had gathered his disciples in a kind of outdoor classroom to give them instructions on how to effectively change the course of human history. Jesus' mission was to offer new hope and redemption. It was a plan for personal and social change that would bring healing, reconciliation, and peace.

To call people "the salt of the earth" is a high compliment. You can depend on such people. They are consistent in their faith and give quiet service to others. But when Jesus told his disciples that they were the salt of the earth, it was more than a compliment; it was a call to a mission. They were to be effective agents of change.

Salt gives taste to bland food and brings out subtle flavours in other foods. It also penetrates food and preserves it. Calling his followers the salt of the earth shows that Jesus expected them to make a difference in a world where people's lives were bland and there seemed no point to living, where gross habits obscured subtle thought and feeling, and where nothing seemed to have lasting value. Jesus' followers were to be the agents by which the world would be transformed and redeemed.

What does it take to be the salt of the earth? I'm sure the disciples of Jesus, when they heard the extreme moral demands of the Sermon on the Mount — to love your enemies, to turn the other cheek, to stop judging others — must have felt that they could never qualify. But earlier in the Sermon on the Mount is a list of very interesting people. We call it the beatitudes. Although in some people's minds it's a list of losers and do-gooders, in Jesus' mind it describes the very people who can make a difference to the world. These are the salt of the earth. These are, for Jesus, highly effective people.

Jesus says, "Blessed are the poor in spirit." Actually, in the version of the Sermon on the Mount found in St. Luke's gospel, Jesus says simply, "Blessed are you who are poor." In both versions, these people are in desperate need and aren't afraid to admit it. They know they have nothing they can call their own — money, a house, a car; great thoughts, great skills, great minds. They know they aren't perfect and haven't got all the answers. They realize they have much to learn and are willing to be taught.

Sometimes at a food bank or a drop-in centre, you may notice a person who is warmly cheerful, who is kind and generous in spite of having very little, and who seems to have unusual and compassionate insight into people. Sometimes a person with these qualities takes a seat on a company board of directors. When you meet such a person, you are in the presence of one of the poor in spirit, one of those salt-of-the-earth agents of change, which Jesus wants his followers to be. To such a person the kingdom of heaven is open.

Jesus goes on, "Blessed are those who mourn" — people who have experienced loss and endured pain, and have neither buried nor denied it. They have cried their way to new courage and new spiritual energy, along with a new compassion and sensitivity for others. In the language of Henri Nouwen, these are the wounded healers. In healing, "they will be comforted."

"Blessed are the meek" — people who don't have to be, or want to be, number one. The meek are those who can live without titles, without prestige, even without recognition. In Peter C. Newman's book, *The Titans*, he lists the names and achievements of the people in this country who are the new movers and shakers of our business culture. But Newman says that these new young Titans are lethal when crossed, terminally self-absorbed and impossible to satisfy." Jesus says that, when it comes to building his kingdom, he'll take the meek any day. "They will inherit the earth."

Jesus' list continues: those who hunger and thirst for righteousness, the merciful, the pure in heart, the peacemakers, those who are persecuted for righteousness sake. These are God's highly effective people. They are his saints, his salt for the earth. It is in the lives of people like this that we see the face of God. They are the people who really make a difference.

Sometimes they appear in positions of power, like Moses in the Bible. Raised with a silver spoon in his mouth, he murdered a soldier and ran for his life, poor in spirit and with much to mourn. Yet God chose him and equipped him to liberate his people and transform them into a great nation. We can think of Nelson Mandela, thirsting for righteousness and justice, spending years in prison, mourning a failed marriage, and then as President of South Africa acting with mercy and striving for peace with justice.

But salt-of-the-earth people are to be found in the most ordinary places: the nurse in the hospital who stays after the end of her shift to make sure that the doctor knows of the change in a patient's condition; the son or daughter who gives up valued weekends to care for an elderly parent; the neighbour who goes in each day to sit with the old man who lives alone. In fact, when Jesus chose his twelve disciples, he didn't conduct a search at the Jerusalem College for Pharisees, seeking the brightest and the best. Instead, he went to a tax collector, fishermen, and other ordinary people whom he knew were poor in spirit, not sure of what they could do but hunger for God. He said to them "follow me" and, as two thousand years of history have shown, they turned the world upside down.

Jesus says to us, "I call you to be the salt of the earth, people who will be effective agents of change. You don't have to be rich, powerful, good-looking, brilliant, or popular. I'm looking for people who are poor in spirit, understand suffering, don't necessarily want to get ahead, are merciful and passionate about justice and peace. Through you I will transform the world."

*Can you recall characteristics or reactions*
*in yourself that you regard as weak?*

*Ask God to show you how these weaknesses*
*can become a blessing.*

❧ ❧

*O Lord, Christ Jesus,*
*who blessed the poor in spirit, the mourners, and the meek:*
*help me to seek the way, the truth, and the life,*
*and to work for righteousness and peace,*
*so that my salt may keep its savour*
*and your spirit fill the world;*
*in your name, I ask.*
*Amen.*

# 11

# Finding the
# Spiritual Thermals

*In the morning, while it was still very dark, Jesus got up and
went out to a deserted place, and there he prayed.*

— Mark 1:35

A few Sundays ago, after attending the early Eucharist at the
cathedral, I made a quick trip to our local Chapters bookstore
to buy some Starbucks coffee. To my surprise, even at that early
hour the store was populated with people quietly browsing in
the aisles. What caught my attention was that the atmosphere
was not unlike church: quiet, reverent, full of serious thought.
If you wanted them, there were ample supplies of spiritual self-
help books — Chicken Soup for just about everybody's soul —
and of course, the best of coffee. It occurred to me that here was
one of the new secular options for Sunday morning spirituality,

and I left wondering what kind of spiritual renewal and what kind of redemptive community the Chapters' Starbucks experience delivers.

St. Mark offers us another option in his description of another Sunday morning experience. He says, "In the morning, while it was still very dark, Jesus got up and went out to a deserted place, and there he prayed." There are pictures in Mark's words: got up, went out (careful not to let the door slam), a deserted place (away from noise and people), and prayer. Perhaps, Jesus went where he could see the coming dawn over the Sea of Galilee and prayed there. In the following verses, Mark describes what Jesus' week was going to be like: "He went throughout Galilee, proclaiming the message in their synagogues and casting out demons." But in order to do that — to bring change and healing to people's lives — Jesus needed his quiet Sunday morning time alone with God in prayer.

Some of us are old enough to remember a time when over half the population of our country spent their Sunday morning in churches. Times have changed. In his book, *The Horizontal Society*, lawyer-sociologist Lawrence Friedman describes a change that has occurred over the last thirty years. The majority of people now draw their identity, their values, and their inspiration for life from beside them and around them. Peer influences have surpassed parental and institutional influences. In this change, vertical authorities, such as families, schools, and religion have lost much of their influence. As a result, people no longer look up to authority figures, such as teachers, parents, police, and clergy.

In such a culture, people looking for spiritual depth in life naturally shy away from the old vertical authority of church and temple, and instead opt for horizontal and peer inspiration. The question is, Does it work? Do the secular options of a quiet bookstore, two hours at the fitness centre, or brunch at a favourite restaurant give you the insight and spiritual energy you need to deal with the work and stress of another week?

All of this brings us to the value of what we call worship, that act of getting up on a Sunday morning, going out of house or apartment, entering a sacred place, and there encountering the spirit of God in prayer. A wonderful promise in Isaiah (40:31) suggests that an encounter with God makes it possible to do things that horizontal living cannot provide: "Those who wait for the Lord shall renew their strength; they shall mount up with wings like eagles, they shall run and not be weary, they shall walk and not faint." These people are not waiting on some horizontal deity. This is the transcendent Creator of the universe. "Have you not heard? The Lord is the everlasting God, the Creator of the ends of the earth. He does not faint, or grow weary; his understanding is unsearchable. He gives power to the faint and strengthens the powerless" (Isaiah 40:28–29).

*National Post* writer Ian Hunter says, "Man was made for worship. If man cannot worship God, then country. If not country, then art. If not art, then he worships himself and that way lies madness and ruin." As a species, we are made to bow down before the infinitely great. Deprived of the infinitely great, our soul seeks lesser sources of inspiration, until it shrivels up and dies of despair.

I suggest to you that the four Sunday morning moves that Jesus made are the four steps to our worship experience with him. First, getting up early in the morning, not just out of obligation but out of need and expectation. Second, going out and leaving what is familiar, usual, and comfortable. Third, going to a sacred place where the conditions are right for communion with God. And fourth, praying and opening ourselves to the renewing empowering energy of God's spirit.

My eldest child, now in his early thirties and a teacher in Toronto, has adopted the rather exotic sport of hang gliding. Strapped under a twenty-five foot wing, the flier either runs off a cliff to become airborne or is towed up by a small aircraft. Joe describes it as a profoundly spiritual experience. Once last summer he was towed up by an ultralight plane and glided over central Ontario at about six thousand feet for almost two hours. I asked how he stayed up so long, given gravity and weight. "Oh," he said, "I look for the birds that are climbing without effort. That's where the thermals are. You have to catch a thermal, an updraft of warm air, and then you can soar like an eagle."

All of us who live in a very horizontal world, who want more than what our peer group can give us and long for an experience of transcendence, need to go where the thermals are … to those sacred places where God is to be found in worship and prayer. It is in these places, as we "wait for the Lord," that our strength is renewed, that we mount up with wings like eagles, run and not grow weary, walk and do not faint.

*Recall some special moment in your life*
*that was beyond and above all others.*

*How could this moment reveal to you*
*the presence of God?*

*O God, our creator,*
*guiding ever faithfully your people down the ages:*
*let me be alert to the light of your presence,*
*so that by searching I may find you,*
*and by finding I may live in you;*
*through Christ, our Lord.*
*Amen.*

# 12

# What is Heaven?

*In my Father's house are many dwelling places. If it were not so, would I have told you that I go to prepare a place for you? And if I go and prepare a place for you, I will come again and will take you to myself, so that where I am, there you may be also.*

— John 14:2–3

I remember the cover of an American magazine that featured a picture of a man standing on a cloud. Underneath the picture were the words, "Does Heaven exist?" It's a fair question these days. Walking out of a Christian funeral service not long ago, I heard one woman say to another, "Oh, I so wish I could believe that stuff about heaven, but it's very hard."

The contemporary world is showing a new fascination with life after death. We hear stories of people who have technically died and been resuscitated. These people speak of passing into a new existence where there is great light, a sense of warmth, and profound love. Brought back suddenly to this present life, they often suffer severe disappointment, even depression, because the other world was so much to be preferred.

For many years now, the church has been noticeably silent on the subject of heaven, apart from derogatory references to "pie in the sky when we die." This hasn't always been so. In the middle ages, when life was filled with poverty, hard labour, and pain, St. Bernard of Cluny drew appealing pictures of heaven in his famous hymn, "Jerusalem the Golden." It was a land of "milk and honey" whose pastures were "decked in glorious sheen." It was a royal hall of feasting where could be heard "the shout of them that triumph, the song of them that feast."

Perhaps our silence on heaven is a kind of twentieth-century reaction against such images. Life on earth is more comfortable for more people now than ever before in history. Instead of looking forward to release in the pastures of the blessed, we can seek self-fulfillment in this present life. The church now places a fresh emphasis on social justice and feeding the hungry — on responding to the needs of people in the here and now. The kingdom of God is seen as something to be experienced while we live rather than after we die.

But things may be changing again. We are a culture that has become disillusioned with the ability of the welfare state to provide paradise on earth. The promises of education, science, business, and government to build the new Jerusalem here and now ring hollow for many people. Some have abandoned the quest for justice and equality, and have made selfishness their rule of life. Others are wondering if there is more to living than can be seen with the eyes.

The biblical witness is clear. "In my Father's house there are many dwelling places. If it were not so, would I have told you that I go to prepare a place for you? And if I go and prepare a place for you, I will come again and will take you to myself, so that where I am, there you may be also." Jesus is saying to his disciples that death is not the end of life, and that he is present for them and for us in what lies beyond life.

St. Paul, in his first letter to the Corinthians, tackles a question that many were asking in his time and many of us ask now. He says, "How can some of you say there is no resurrection of the dead? If there is no resurrection of the dead, then Christ has not been raised.... If Christ has not been raised, your faith is futile.... But someone will ask, 'How are the dead raised? With what kind of body do they come?' Fool! What you sow does not come to life unless it dies.... You do not sow the body that is to be, but a bare seed.... God gives it a body as he has chosen.... What is sown is perishable, what is raised is imperisable.... It is sown a physical body, it is raised a spiritual body.... Flesh and blood cannot inherit the kingdom of God, nor does the perishable inherit the imperishable.... When this perishable body puts on imperishability ... then ... death has been swallowed up in victory." To stress the reality of heaven, Paul avoids pie in the sky images, preferring the homely image of sowing seed.

By contrast, one of the most impressive images of heaven comes from a vision that St. John records in the Book of Revelation. "After this I looked, and there was a great multitude that no one could count, from every nation, from all tribes and peoples and languages, standing before the throne.... They will hunger no more and thirst no more ... for the Lamb at the centre of the throne will be their shepherd, and he will guide them to springs of the water of life, and God will wipe away every tear from their eyes."

All of the biblical writers acknowledge that, when they speak of things beyond this life, they see them "through a glass darkly." Heaven is a mystery. But they write with the conviction that God hasn't created us just to get sick and die and that's the end. Nor do they suggest that the soul somehow escapes and is reincarnated somewhere else. No. They insist there is real death, but that beyond physical existence lies a spiritual reality where we will be made new, and where every tear will be wiped away.

Last year, a new book came out by Jeffrey Russell called *History of Heaven.* He says, "Heaven is not something that begins after we die. We can taste it even now by knowing him who rules there. Heaven is not dull. It is not static. It is an endless dynamic of joy, in which one is ever more oneself, as one was meant to be."

C.S. Lewis once wrote, "Heaven is the secret we cannot hide and cannot tell.... We cannot tell it because it is a desire for something that has never actually appeared in our experience. We cannot hide it because our experience is constantly suggesting it."

A story is told of John Todd, a clergyman. When he was six years old both his parents died, and a kind-hearted aunt raised him until he went to seminary. Many years later, old and ill and in distress, she wrote him a letter wondering what death would mean and if there was anything beyond it.

He wrote back, "It has now been thirty years since I came to you, dear aunt. When my parents died, you sent word that you would give me a home and care for me. I remember coming on the train alone. Your man met me. I climbed on his horse behind him for the journey through the darkness. I was afraid, lonely. I said to him, 'Do you think she'll be in bed when we get there?' 'Oh no,' he said, 'she'll be up for you. There'll be a candle in the window.' Presently we came into a clearing and there, sure enough, was a light in the window.

"I remember you waiting for me at the door, your arms open for me. You had a fire burning, a hot supper waiting on the stove. After supper, you took me to my new room, heard me say my prayers and sat there until I fell asleep. Some day, dear aunt, God will send for you to take you to a new home. Don't fear the summons, the mysterious journey. God can be trusted to do as much for you as you were kind enough to do for me. At the end of the road you will find love and a welcome awaiting, a candle in the window and you will be safe. Safer than you ever have been, in God's care."

You and I were not created just to get sick, suffer, and die. There is more to God than that. There is more to us than that. We see it now only through a "glass darkly," but then we will see him "face to face" where, in the words of John Donne, "there no darkness nor dazzling, but one equal light; no noise nor silence, but one equal music; no fear nor hopes, but one equal possession; no ends nor beginnings, but one equal eternity."

*Imagine what it would be like*
*to be surrounded by those whom you most love.*

*What do you think it would be like*
*to rest in the presence of God?*

*O Lord, Christ Jesus,*
*who opened the kingdom of heaven to all believers:*
*let me so build your kingdom here on earth*
*that all my days may be a preparation*
*to enter your kingdom in heaven;*
*in your name, I ask.*
*Amen.*

**Path Books**
A LIGHT TO MY PATH

We hope that you have enjoyed reading this Path Book. For more information about Path Books, please visit our website at **www.pathbooks.com**. If you have comments or suggestions about Path Books, please write to us at **publisher@pathbooks.com.**

## *Other Path Books*

**Practical Prayer: Making Space for God in Everyday Life** by Anne Tanner. A richly textured presentation of the history, practices, and implications of Christian prayer and meditation to help people live a rewarding life in a stressful world.
*1-55126-321-1 $18.95*

Also available: *Prayer: Leader's Resources*, a booklet for study groups, and *Practical Prayer: An Exercise in Contemplative Prayer*, a cassette tape on meditation practice.

**Prayer Companion: A Treasury of Personal Meditation** by Judith Lawrence. A personal prayer resource providing gems for daily living, meditation, and prayer. A friendly companion to those searching for greater meaning in everyday experience.
*1-55126-319-X $18.95*

*Available from your local bookstore or*
*Anglican Book Centre, phone 1-800-268-1168*
*or write 600 Jarvis Street, Toronto, ON M4Y 2J6*